The
★ ★
UNITED
STATES
PRESIDENTS

  Grover

CLEVELAND

BreAnn Rumsch

Big Buddy Books

An Imprint of Abdo Publishing
abdopublishing.com

abdopublishing.com

Published by Abdo Publishing, a division of ABDO, PO Box 398166, Minneapolis, Minnesota 55439. Copyright © 2017 by Abdo Consulting Group, Inc. International copyrights reserved in all countries. No part of this book may be reproduced in any form without written permission from the publisher. Big Buddy Books™ is a trademark and logo of Abdo Publishing.

Printed in the United States of America, North Mankato, Minnesota
062016
092016

THIS BOOK CONTAINS
RECYCLED MATERIALS

Design: Sarah DeYoung, Mighty Media, Inc.
Production: Mighty Media, Inc.
Editor: Lauren Kukla
Cover Photograph: Getty Images
Interior Photographs: Alamy (pp. 6, 7, 9, 15); AP Images (p. 29); Corbis (pp. 7, 19, 27);
    iStockphoto (p. 17); Library of Congress (pp. 5, 21, 23, 25); National Portrait Gallery,
    Smithsonian Institution / Art Resource (p. 13); Picture History (p. 11)

Cataloging-in-Publication Data

Names: Rumsch, BreAnn, author.
Title: Grover Cleveland / by BreAnn Rumsch.
Description: Minneapolis, MN : Abdo Publishing, [2017] | Series: United States
    presidents | Includes bibliographical references and index.
Identifiers: LCCN 2015045521 | ISBN 9781680780888 (lib. bdg.) |
    ISBN 9781680775082 (ebook)
Subjects: LCSH: Cleveland, Grover, 1837-1908--Juvenile literature. 2.
    Presidents--United States--Biography--Juvenile literature. | United States--
    Politics and Government--1885-1889--Juvenile literature. | United States--
    Politics and Government--1893-1897--Juvenile literature.
Classification: DDC 973.8/5092092 [B]--dc23
LC record available at http://lccn.loc.gov/2015045521

Contents

Grover Cleveland 4

Timeline 6

Young Grover 8

New York Lawyer 10

The Veto Mayor 14

President Cleveland 18

Early Retirement 22

Back in Office 26

Final Retirement 28

Office of the President 30

Presidents and Their Terms 34

Glossary 38

Websites 39

Index 40

Grover Cleveland

Grover Cleveland was the twenty-second and twenty-fourth US president. He is the only president whose terms were not in a row.

In 1884, Cleveland was elected president. Four years later, he ran for reelection and lost. Then, in 1892, Cleveland was elected president for a second time.

As president, Cleveland's leadership was not always popular. But he did what he believed was right for his country. Over time, Americans came to respect his ideas and his honesty.

Timeline

1837

On March 18, Stephen Grover Cleveland was born in Caldwell, New Jersey.

1885

On March 4, Cleveland became the twenty-second US president.

1883

On January 3, Cleveland became governor of New York.

1888

Cleveland lost reelection.

1897

Cleveland moved to Princeton, New Jersey.

1893

On March 4, Cleveland became the twenty-fourth US president.

1908

Grover Cleveland died on June 24.

7

Young Grover

Stephen Grover Cleveland was born in Caldwell, New Jersey, on March 18, 1837. His family called him Grover. In 1853, Grover's father died.

After his father's death, Grover had to help provide for his family. So, he got a teaching job at a school for the blind.

Grover's birthplace was in Caldwell, New Jersey, but he spent much of his childhood living in New York.

New York Lawyer

In 1854, Cleveland moved to Buffalo, New York. He began learning as much as he could about law. He read many law books and watched **lawyers** at work.

In Buffalo, Cleveland also became interested in **politics**. In 1865, he worked on **Democrat** James Buchanan's presidential campaign. Buchanan won the election. From then on, Cleveland considered himself a member of the Democratic Party.

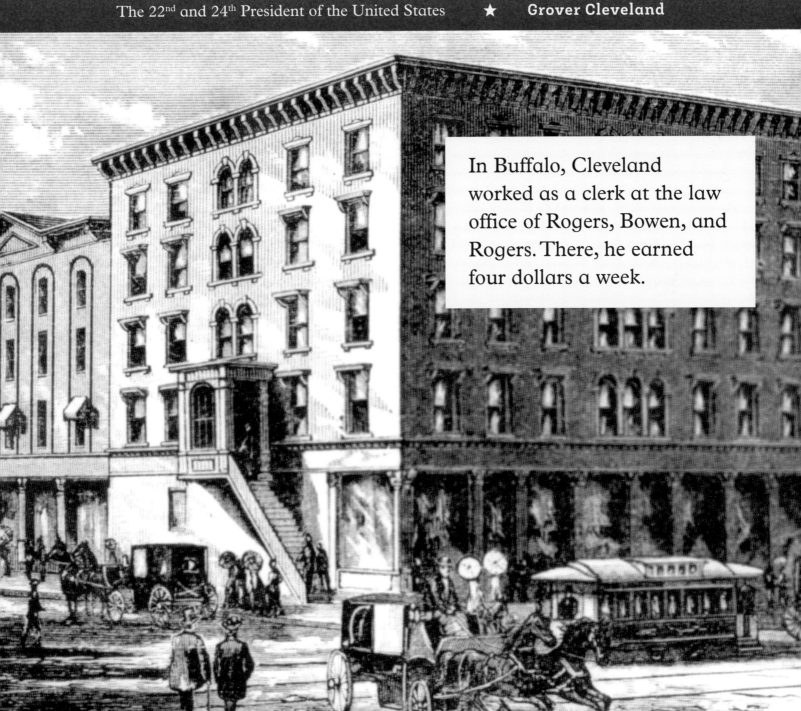

In Buffalo, Cleveland worked as a clerk at the law office of Rogers, Bowen, and Rogers. There, he earned four dollars a week.

In 1859, Cleveland passed the test to become a **lawyer**. Then in 1863, he became **assistant district attorney** of Erie County, New York.

Meanwhile, the **American Civil War** was being fought. In May 1863, Cleveland was selected to serve in the war. However, he was providing for his mother and sisters. So, Cleveland hired someone to go to war for him.

From 1870 to 1873, Cleveland served as **sheriff** of Erie County. Then, he practiced law in Buffalo.

★ DID YOU KNOW? ★

As assistant district attorney, Cleveland would often work in his office until three o'clock in the morning.

Cleveland was a successful assistant district attorney. Some days, he won all of his cases!

The Veto Mayor

In 1881, Cleveland ran for mayor of Buffalo. He won the election! As mayor, he **vetoed** many dishonest bills. Cleveland became known as the Veto Mayor.

Cleveland's honest character became more well-known. In 1882, he was chosen to run for governor of New York. He won the election.

On January 3, 1883, Cleveland took office. As governor, he kept his honest approach to work. Cleveland did not grant special favors or make secret deals.

Outside Buffalo city hall stands a bronze statue of Cleveland.

The **Democratic** Party had high hopes for Cleveland. In 1884, Democrats chose Cleveland to run for president. The **Republicans** chose James G. Blaine.

However, many Republicans distrusted Blaine. They refused to vote for him. Instead, they voted for Cleveland.

It was a very close election. There was no clear winner at first. The votes had to be recounted. In the end, Cleveland won.

★ DID YOU KNOW? ★

The Republicans who voted for Cleveland were known as mugwumps.

As governor, Cleveland signed a bill to preserve the land around Niagara Falls in New York. This land later became a state park.

President Cleveland

Cleveland was **inaugurated** on March 4, 1885. His first task was to name his **cabinet** and fill **civil service** jobs. New presidents usually choose people from their own **political** party. This is called the spoils system.

But Cleveland did not agree with the spoils system. So, he chose the best people for the jobs, whether they were **Democrats** or not.

★ SUPREME COURT APPOINTMENTS ★

Lucius Q.C. Lamar: 1888

Melville Weston Fuller: 1888

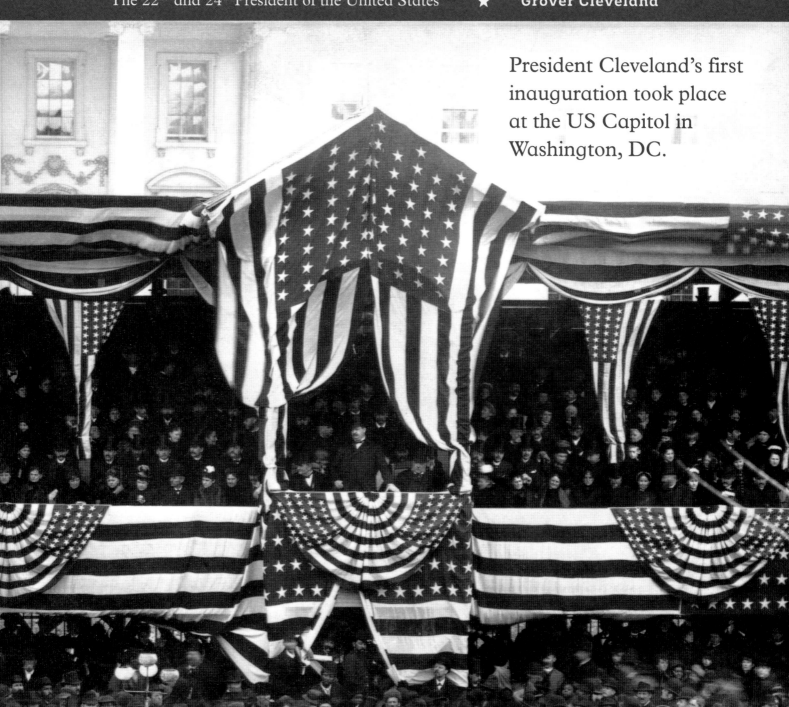

President Cleveland's first inauguration took place at the US Capitol in Washington, DC.

On November 25, 1885, Vice President Thomas A. Hendricks died. Cleveland worried about who would be president if he died too. So, in January 1886, he asked Congress to pass an act to solve this problem. The act stated who would lead the country if the president and vice president could not.

Then, in February 1887, Cleveland signed an act that gave land and US citizenship to Native Americans. But first, they had to give up their **reservation** land.

> ★ DID YOU KNOW? ★
>
> The United States received the Statue of Liberty from France during Cleveland's presidency.

Cleveland married Frances Folsom on June 2, 1886. He was the first president to get married in the White House.

Early Retirement

Cleveland ran for reelection in 1888. He ran against **Republican** Benjamin Harrison. The election of 1888 was one of the most unusual in US history.

President Cleveland won about 100,000 more **popular votes** than Harrison. However, Harrison had 233 **electoral votes** to Cleveland's 168. So, Harrison won the election.

In March 1889, the Clevelands left the White House. They moved to New York City. Cleveland worked there as a **lawyer**.

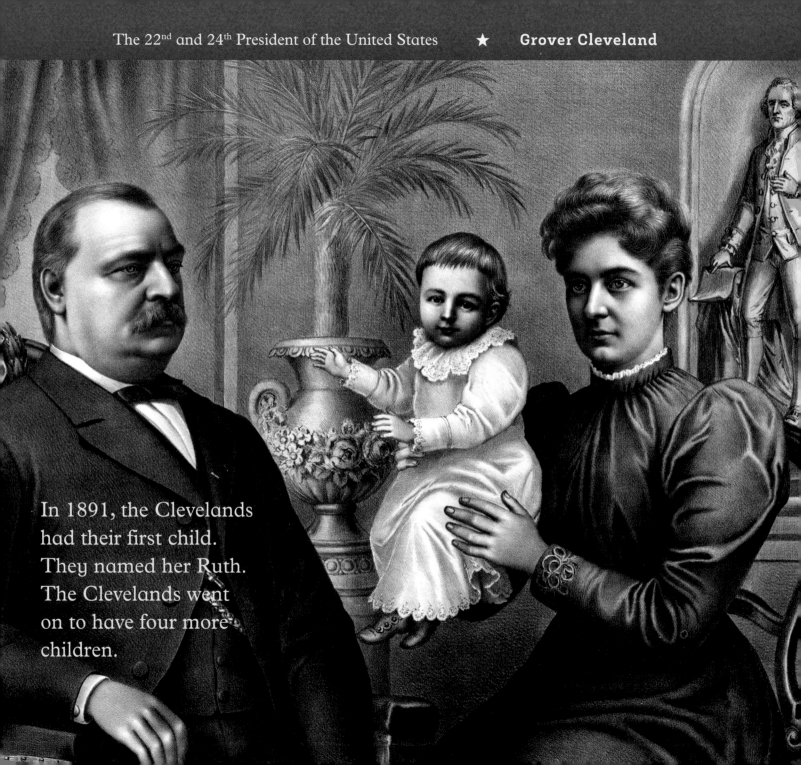

In 1891, the Clevelands had their first child. They named her Ruth. The Clevelands went on to have four more children.

Congress had passed the Sherman Silver Purchase Act in 1890. It increased the amount of silver the government purchased each month. Cleveland spoke out against the act. He believed the **gold standard** system was better for the country.

Many **Democrats** disagreed with Cleveland. However, he was still chosen to run for president in 1892. The **Republicans** chose President Harrison.

During the campaign, President Harrison sent troops to stop a strike in Pennsylvania. This angered many Americans. So, Cleveland easily won the election.

Benjamin Harrison
was president of
the United States
from 1889 to 1893.

Back in Office

Cleveland began his second term on March 4, 1893. In May of that year, a **depression** began. President Cleveland blamed the Sherman Silver Purchase Act. He worked with Congress to cancel the act.

As the depression continued, Americans became angry. A major strike happened in Chicago, Illinois, in 1894. Due to the strike, the US mail could not be delivered. So, Cleveland sent troops to stop the strike. This pleased businesses, but many workers didn't like it.

PRESIDENT CLEVELAND'S CABINET

First Term
March 4, 1885–March 4, 1889

★ **STATE:** Thomas F. Bayard
★ **TREASURY:** Daniel Manning,
Charles S. Fairchild (from April 1, 1887)
★ **WAR:** William C. Endicott
★ **NAVY:** William C. Whitney
★ **ATTORNEY GENERAL:** Augustus H. Garland
★ **INTERIOR:** Lucius Q.C. Lamar,
William F. Vilas (from January 16, 1888)
★ **AGRICULTURE:** Norman J. Colman
(from February 3, 1889)

Second Term
March 4, 1893–March 4, 1897

★ **STATE:** Walter Q. Gresham,
Richard Olney (from June 10, 1895)
★ **TREASURY:** John G. Carlisle
★ **WAR:** Daniel S. Lamont
★ **NAVY:** Hilary A. Herbert
★ **ATTORNEY GENERAL:** Richard Olney,
Judson Harmon (from June 11, 1895)
★ **INTERIOR:** Hoke Smith, David R. Francis
(from September 4, 1896)
★ **AGRICULTURE:** J. Sterling Morton

Final Retirement

The next election was in 1896. Many **Democrats** were ready for a new **candidate**. Cleveland was also ready to leave the White House.

Cleveland's presidency ended in March 1897. He and his family moved to Princeton, New Jersey. Cleveland died there on June 24, 1908.

Grover Cleveland brought honesty and honor to all of his public offices. Some of Cleveland's beliefs made him unpopular. However, he always stood up for what he thought was right.

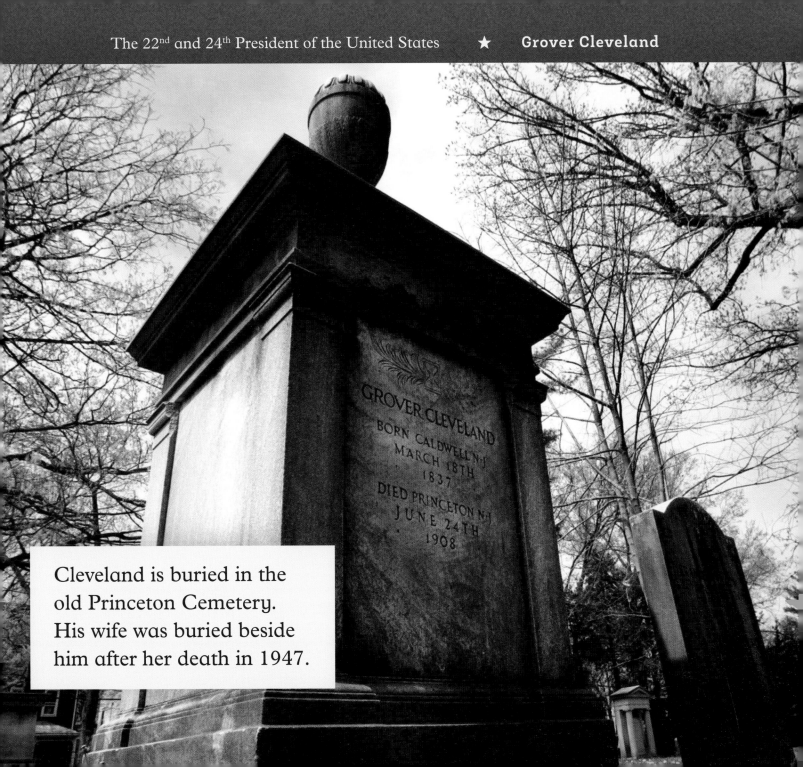

GROVER CLEVELAND
BORN CALDWELL N.J
MARCH 18TH
1837

DIED PRINCETON N.J
JUNE 24TH
1908

Cleveland is buried in the old Princeton Cemetery. His wife was buried beside him after her death in 1947.

Office of the President

Branches of Government

The US government has three branches. They are the executive, legislative, and judicial branches. Each branch has some power over the others. This is called a system of checks and balances.

★ Executive Branch

The executive branch enforces laws. It is made up of the president, the vice president, and the president's cabinet. The president represents the United States around the world. He or she also signs bills into law and leads the military.

★ Legislative Branch

The legislative branch makes laws, maintains the military, and regulates trade. It also has the power to declare war. This branch includes the Senate and the House of Representatives. Together, these two houses form Congress.

★ Judicial Branch

The judicial branch interprets laws. It is made up of district courts, courts of appeals, and the Supreme Court. District courts try cases. Sometimes people disagree with a trial's outcome. Then he or she may appeal. If a court of appeals supports the ruling, a person may appeal to the Supreme Court.

Qualifications for Office

To be president, a candidate must be at least 35 years old. The person must be a natural-born US citizen. He or she must also have lived in the United States for at least 14 years.

Electoral College

The US presidential election is an indirect election. Voters from each state choose electors. These electors represent their state in the Electoral College. Each elector has one electoral vote. Electors cast their vote for the candidate with the highest number of votes from people in their state. A candidate must receive the majority of Electoral College votes to win.

Term of Office

Each president may be elected to two four-year terms. The presidential election is held on the Tuesday after the first Monday in November. The president is sworn in on January 20 of the following year. At that time, he or she takes the oath of office.
It states:

> I do solemnly swear (or affirm) that I will faithfully execute the office of President of the United States, and will to the best of my ability, preserve, protect and defend the Constitution of the United States.

31

Line of Succession

The Presidential Succession Act of 1947 states who becomes president if the president cannot serve. The vice president is first in the line. Next are the Speaker of the House and the President Pro Tempore of the Senate. It may happen that none of these individuals is able to serve. Then the office falls to the president's cabinet members. They would take office in the order in which each department was created:

Secretary of State

Secretary of the Treasury

Secretary of Defense

Attorney General

Secretary of the Interior

Secretary of Agriculture

Secretary of Commerce

Secretary of Labor

Secretary of Health and Human Services

Secretary of Housing and Urban Development

Secretary of Transportation

Secretary of Energy

Secretary of Education

Secretary of Veterans Affairs

Secretary of Homeland Security

Benefits

★ While in office, the president receives a salary. It is $400,000 per year. He or she lives in the White House. The president also has 24-hour Secret Service protection.

★ The president may travel on a Boeing 747 jet. This special jet is called Air Force One. It can hold 70 passengers. It has kitchens, a dining room, sleeping areas, and more. Air Force One can fly halfway around the world before needing to refuel. It can even refuel in flight!

★ When the president travels by car, he or she uses Cadillac One. It is a Cadillac Deville that has been modified. The car has heavy armor and communications systems. The president may even take Cadillac One along when visiting other countries.

★ The president also travels on a helicopter. It is called Marine One. It may also be taken along when the president visits other countries.

★ Sometimes the president needs to get away with family and friends. Camp David is the official presidential retreat. It is located in Maryland. The US Navy maintains the retreat. The US Marine Corps keeps it secure. The camp offers swimming, tennis, golf, and hiking.

★ When the president leaves office, he or she receives lifetime Secret Service protection. He or she also receives a yearly pension of $203,700. The former president also receives money for office space, supplies, and staff.

PRESIDENTS AND THEIR TERMS

PRESIDENT	PARTY	TOOK OFFICE	LEFT OFFICE	TERMS SERVED	VICE PRESIDENT
George Washington	None	April 30, 1789	March 4, 1797	Two	John Adams
John Adams	Federalist	March 4, 1797	March 4, 1801	One	Thomas Jefferson
Thomas Jefferson	Democratic-Republican	March 4, 1801	March 4, 1809	Two	Aaron Burr, George Clinton
James Madison	Democratic-Republican	March 4, 1809	March 4, 1817	Two	George Clinton, Elbridge Gerry
James Monroe	Democratic-Republican	March 4, 1817	March 4, 1825	Two	Daniel D. Tompkins
John Quincy Adams	Democratic-Republican	March 4, 1825	March 4, 1829	One	John C. Calhoun
Andrew Jackson	Democrat	March 4, 1829	March 4, 1837	Two	John C. Calhoun, Martin Van Buren
Martin Van Buren	Democrat	March 4, 1837	March 4, 1841	One	Richard M. Johnson
William H. Harrison	Whig	March 4, 1841	April 4, 1841	Died During First Term	John Tyler
John Tyler	Whig	April 6, 1841	March 4, 1845	Completed Harrison's Term	Office Vacant
James K. Polk	Democrat	March 4, 1845	March 4, 1849	One	George M. Dallas
Zachary Taylor	Whig	March 5, 1849	July 9, 1850	Died During First Term	Millard Fillmore

PRESIDENT	PARTY	TOOK OFFICE	LEFT OFFICE	TERMS SERVED	VICE PRESIDENT
Millard Fillmore	Whig	July 10, 1850	March 4, 1853	Completed Taylor's Term	Office Vacant
Franklin Pierce	Democrat	March 4, 1853	March 4, 1857	One	William R.D. King
James Buchanan	Democrat	March 4, 1857	March 4, 1861	One	John C. Breckinridge
Abraham Lincoln	Republican	March 4, 1861	April 15, 1865	Served One Term, Died During Second Term	Hannibal Hamlin, Andrew Johnson
Andrew Johnson	Democrat	April 15, 1865	March 4, 1869	Completed Lincoln's Second Term	Office Vacant
Ulysses S. Grant	Republican	March 4, 1869	March 4, 1877	Two	Schuyler Colfax, Henry Wilson
Rutherford B. Hayes	Republican	March 3, 1877	March 4, 1881	One	William A. Wheeler
James A. Garfield	Republican	March 4, 1881	September 19, 1881	Died During First Term	Chester Arthur
Chester Arthur	Republican	September 20, 1881	March 4, 1885	Completed Garfield's Term	Office Vacant
Grover Cleveland	Democrat	March 4, 1885	March 4, 1889	One	Thomas A. Hendricks
Benjamin Harrison	Republican	March 4, 1889	March 4, 1893	One	Levi P. Morton
Grover Cleveland	Democrat	March 4, 1893	March 4, 1897	One	Adlai E. Stevenson
William McKinley	Republican	March 4, 1897	September 14, 1901	Served One Term, Died During Second Term	Garret A. Hobart, Theodore Roosevelt

PRESIDENT	PARTY	TOOK OFFICE	LEFT OFFICE	TERMS SERVED	VICE PRESIDENT
Theodore Roosevelt	Republican	September 14, 1901	March 4, 1909	Completed McKinley's Second Term, Served One Term	Office Vacant, Charles Fairbanks
William Taft	Republican	March 4, 1909	March 4, 1913	One	James S. Sherman
Woodrow Wilson	Democrat	March 4, 1913	March 4, 1921	Two	Thomas R. Marshall
Warren G. Harding	Republican	March 4, 1921	August 2, 1923	Died During First Term	Calvin Coolidge
Calvin Coolidge	Republican	August 3, 1923	March 4, 1929	Completed Harding's Term, Served One Term	Office Vacant, Charles Dawes
Herbert Hoover	Republican	March 4, 1929	March 4, 1933	One	Charles Curtis
Franklin D. Roosevelt	Democrat	March 4, 1933	April 12, 1945	Served Three Terms, Died During Fourth Term	John Nance Garner, Henry A. Wallace, Harry S. Truman
Harry S. Truman	Democrat	April 12, 1945	January 20, 1953	Completed Roosevelt's Fourth Term, Served One Term	Office Vacant, Alben Barkley
Dwight D. Eisenhower	Republican	January 20, 1953	January 20, 1961	Two	Richard Nixon
John F. Kennedy	Democrat	January 20, 1961	November 22, 1963	Died During First Term	Lyndon B. Johnson
Lyndon B. Johnson	Democrat	November 22, 1963	January 20, 1969	Completed Kennedy's Term, Served One Term	Office Vacant, Hubert H. Humphrey
Richard Nixon	Republican	January 20, 1969	August 9, 1974	Completed First Term, Resigned During Second Term	Spiro T. Agnew, Gerald Ford

PRESIDENT	PARTY	TOOK OFFICE	LEFT OFFICE	TERMS SERVED	VICE PRESIDENT
Gerald Ford	Republican	August 9, 1974	January 20, 1977	Completed Nixon's Second Term	Nelson A. Rockefeller
Jimmy Carter	Democrat	January 20, 1977	January 20, 1981	One	Walter Mondale
Ronald Reagan	Republican	January 20, 1981	January 20, 1989	Two	George H.W. Bush
George H.W. Bush	Republican	January 20, 1989	January 20, 1993	One	Dan Quayle
Bill Clinton	Democrat	January 20, 1993	January 20, 2001	Two	Al Gore
George W. Bush	Republican	January 20, 2001	January 20, 2009	Two	Dick Cheney
Barack Obama	Democrat	January 20, 2009	January 20, 2017	Two	Joe Biden

"I have only one thing to do and that is to do right, and that is easy." Grover Cleveland

★ WRITE TO THE PRESIDENT ★

You may write to the president at:
The White House
1600 Pennsylvania Avenue NW
Washington, DC 20500

You may e-mail the president at:
comments@whitehouse.gov

37

Glossary

American Civil War—the war between the Northern and Southern states from 1861 to 1865.

assistant district attorney—a person who gives the government advice on laws and works in a specific district, such as a county or a state.

cabinet—a group of advisers chosen by the president to lead government departments.

candidate (KAN-duh-dayt)—a person who seeks a political office.

civil service—the part of the government that is responsible for matters not covered by the military, the courts, or the law.

Democrat—a member of the Democratic political party.

depression—a period of economic trouble when there is little buying or selling and many people are out of work.

electoral vote—a vote cast by a member of the Electoral College for the candidate who received the most popular votes in his or her state.

gold standard—a system in which the dollar is equal to a certain amount of gold.

inaugurate—to swear into a political office.

lawyer (LAW-yuhr)—a person who gives people advice on laws or represents them in court.

politics—the art or science of government. Something referring to politics is political. A person who is active in politics is a politician.

popular vote—the vote of the entire body of people with the right to vote.

Republican—a member of the Republican political party.

reservation (reh-zuhr-VAY-shuhn)—a piece of land set aside by the government for Native Americans to live on.

sheriff—the highest-ranking law officer in a county.

veto—the right of one member of a decision-making group to stop an action by the group. In the US government, the president can veto bills passed by Congress. But Congress can override the president's veto if two-thirds of its members vote to do so.

★ WEBSITES ★

To learn more about the US Presidents, visit **booklinks.abdopublishing.com**. These links are routinely monitored and updated to provide the most current information available.

Index

American Civil War **12**

birth **6, 8, 9**

Blaine, James G. **16**

Buchanan, James **10**

childhood **8, 9**

death **7, 8, 28, 29**

Democratic Party **8, 10, 16, 18, 24, 28**

depression **26**

education **10**

family **8, 12, 21, 23, 28, 29**

gold standard **24**

governor **6, 14, 17**

Harrison, Benjamin **22, 24, 25**

Hendricks, Thomas A. **8, 20**

inauguration **8, 19**

mayor **14**

mugwumps **16**

Native Americans **20**

Niagara Falls **17**

Republican Party **16, 22, 24**

retirement **22, 28**

sheriff **12**

Sherman Silver Purchase Act **24, 26**

spoils system **18**

strikes **24, 26**